Of Cheese and Chutney

Also by Ian McFarlane and published by Ginninderra Press

Evening at Murunna Point

Of Cheese & Chutney

Aspects of Empathy (Pocket Poets)

A Bold Concept (Pocket Polemics)

Of Bluebells & Barbed Wire (Pocket Places)

Other books by Ian McFarlane

The Jerusalem Conspiracy

The Siberian Sparrows

Shadows

Ian McFarlane

Of Cheese and Chutney

Selected essays

GP

For Rob Wilson

Friendship is as friendship does,
and here's to yours and mine;
it grafted young and strengthened,
like fruit upon the vine.

Of Cheese and Chutney: Selected essays
ISBN 978 1 74027 583 5
Copyright © Ian McFarlane 2009

First published in this form 2009
Reprinted 2015

GINNINDERRA PRESS
PO Box 3461 Port Adelaide SA 5015
www.ginninderrapress.com.au

Contents

Just when the Gods had ceased to be, and the Christ had not yet come, there was a unique moment in history, between Cicero and Marcus Aurelius, when Man stood alone.

Gustave Flaubert (1821–1880)

Of cheese and chutney

I've always suspected people who claim to enjoy writing to be working from the wrong imperative. Revision can be pleasant, when it's going well, and you can see an original idea taking shape from the fanciful fuzziness of a first draft, but, for me, the blank page is a terribly barren thing, enough to paralyse the psyche into a curious kind of free-floating fear. The fear T.S. Eliot found in his handful of dust. A fear of nothingness.

So, filling a blank page with words that may or may not be later revisable can be an agonising experience, rather like having a tooth pulled by a clumsy dentist. And this might help explain why, over my working life as a writer, I haven't managed to fill the number of blank pages required to avoid falling off the edge of the literary map. It's not that I don't have anything to say. The trouble is, there's usually far too much. Ideas for essays, scraps of dialogue for stories, bits of poems burnt into existence from existential depression, all rushing down like an avalanche of black fire. And crowding each other into the merciful oblivion of silence.

But there's something else. Which, thanks to a deeply ingrained work ethic, I'm almost ashamed to admit. It's this: I've always rather enjoyed the aesthetic sense of idleness. The truth is, I happen to like sitting at my desk, staring out through a window, with a nice cup of tea and a cheese and chutney sandwich close to hand. Pretending to write. In my defence, it could be said that such elemental quietude seems an appropriate response to the noisily chaotic lack of meaning presently driving our mad, bad world, with its posturing arrogance and vacuous morality, a world where prejudice, hatred and cruelty are fabricated daily in the name of cultural imperialism. Or gods with the same credibility problems as Father Christmas.

As a child, the Bible promised me – poetically, before the awful age of economic rationalism put paid to such profitless pursuits – that things were first seen face to face, but later through a glass darkly. Now, that darkness seduces me into the honey-coated idleness of intensely hopeless reflections, slowly freezing me into a mythical landscape, where tolerance, compassion and justice might have once existed. Where writers were moved by the passion of having something interesting and original to say, not because they'd recently completed a creative writing course, retired with a favourable word processing package, or developed an infatuation for the celebrity cult of authorship.

Let's face it, there are only two kinds of people who write: those who want to, and those who have to. And although it would be difficult to conduct an accurate survey, I'm prepared to accept that the best writing – by virtue of its suppleness of expression combined with a lucid depth of insight – is likely to come from someone who had to do it, rather than someone who merely wanted to. For instance, reading a novel by Thea Astley or Tim Winton is a damned sight more likely to enhance your perception of what it means to be human than reading one by Bryce Courtenay or Colleen McCullough. Why is this? Is it simply a matter of claiming that Thea and Tim are better writers than Bryce and Colleen? Well, no, that's a subjective value judgement, and therefore vulnerable. And anyway, there's more to it than that. Such as the ebb and flow currents between substance and flavour, the cheese and chutney factors of writing, as part of a complex and isolated activity that needs a flute of idleness now and then, as the body needs a flask of water.

Of course, value judgements about any kind of writing are highly subjective. They're also linked to a subtle synergy that must somehow exist between writer and reader, if any book is going to work, whatever its literary intention. And this can have to do with the way a writer regards him or herself in an orbiting galaxy of sometimes brightly lit stars where confidence can wander off into arrogance and reticence become misconstrued as something else. Some writers, usually because they adapt well to aggressive marketing, find themselves accompanied by clusters of supplicant moons in the shape of publicists and patrons, who encourage them to believe that this is the way it is, and – bugger you, Jack – the way it will remain. Others, perhaps for reasons to do with personality, seek less brightly lit regions of the galaxy, maybe a favourably disposed black hole, finding themselves overlooked or ignored, and facing the ethically flimsy prospect of having to turn such misfortune into a virtue, by rejecting celebrity status as a vulgar distraction.

I've never understood our pathetic infatuation with celebrity. Perhaps it has something to do with that bloody handful of dust. Maybe it's the chutney that makes the cheese of life more palatable. Anyway, I'll rest my oars on one last proposition. Writing a book is an act of great presumption, since it presumes someone will find the money, time and effort to read the words. Therefore, a writer's imperative should always be to make the cheese worth the chutney.

Of bombs and bails

Bombs began falling on Baghdad the same evening (Australian time) as the first over was being bowled in South Africa at the World Cup Cricket semi-final between India and Kenya. Channel surfing into the night from one international contest to the other, I began to suffer a slightly surreal cultural dissonance, half-expecting the sliding bar at the bottom of my screen to 'update' me with the breaking news that Iraq was eight down for three runs in the second over, chasing 942 for victory. Or that Kenya was using hollow cricket bats to cleverly conceal its weapons of mass destruction from India's bowlers and UN-appointed umpires.

Growing up in a green and pleasant part of 1950s England, I played a lot of schoolboy cricket, and carried some painful memories of recent war, but only – I hasten to add – as a confused and frightened bystander. A few years earlier, I had sensed something awful was happening when bits of flaming metal began falling from the sky into neighbouring haystacks, but was too young to understand what it all meant.

Half a century on, I'm still not sure, because war is a chaotic and ugly form of madness. Cricket, on the other hand, is (or used to be) a sublimely intricate expression of beauty. As suggested by this fragment of a poem by John Arlott:

> Sunburned fieldsmen, flannelled cream
> Looked, though urgent, scarce alive
> Swooped, like swallows of a dream,
> On skimming fly, the hard-hit drive.

Stand that alongside these lines on war from Wilfred Owen:

> What passing-bells for those who die as cattle?

Only the monstrous anger of the guns,
Only the stuttering rifles' rapid rattle
Can patter out their hasty orisons.

The Duke of Wellington's famous claim that Waterloo was 'won on the playing fields of Eton', and Sir Henry Newbolt's 'breathless hush on the close' poem, opening on a village cricket green, with ten runs to make on a bumping pitch, before fading to a 'regiment blinded by dust and smoke', stirred many a schoolboy's blood, including mine. Patriotism, like the banality of cheap music, has a shrill volume, which the 'coalition of the willing' played loudly, to drown the screams of children being slaughtered by incoming 'smart' bombs.

Cricket and war are unpredictable activities. You never know when a patch of roughed-up turf outside the leg stump will grip sufficiently for your front-line wrist spinner to bowl a mesmerised batsman around his legs. Just as you never know when a highly trained pilot, flying on adrenalin, with combat reactions honed hair-trigger keen, will squeeze the button on a target thought to be dangerous…and incinerate a column of harmless civilians, or bring down 'friendly' fire on a bunch of his ground-force mates. At least the batsman has the option of another innings.

Of course, the politicians and generals would argue that countries go to war for vastly more important reasons than they go to cricket. For example, India was playing Kenya to decide who got to the final against Australia, to play for the World Cup, involving a lot of loot, and the right to be known (and feared) as the strongest team in the world. The 'coalition of the willing' was invading Iraq for the lofty idea of freedom, although the word was spelled with only three letters: o–i–l, and carried a prize involving torrents of loot, as well as the right to be known (and feared) as the strongest team in the world. Spot the important difference?

Cricket has placed its crested blazer and creams in hock for more lucrative plumage and, although war has always dressed for the kill, its increasingly sombre cloth reflects not only a practical need to keep the head down, but also an almost eerie acceptance of its dehumanised reality. The splendidly attired Duke of Wellington, or Napoleon for that matter, would almost certainly have declined any action outside the unwritten code of battlefield honour respected by both sides. John Arlott's sunburned fieldsmen might still be flannelled cream when playing real cricket, but are now more likely to 'sledge' rather than 'swoop', and set a very slack field to slow the rate of quick-scoring greed.

When a recent South African test captain was exposed as a money-grubbing cheat, the purists took it hard. After all, wasn't cricket supposed to be synonymous with honour? It's simply not cricket! was a cry widely accepted as expressing dismay at bad behaviour. Well, in case you hadn't noticed, this tired old world is groaning under the weight of terrible behaviour. Militant consumerism and fundamentalist religion are breeding a new global sickness faster, and more deadly, than a speeding virus. The light is failing, the pitch looks bumpy, and even cricket isn't cricket any more. War is still war. Except that it's just got a damn sight nastier.

Oh well, I guess the best we can do is make sure we all get padded up. And carry hollow bats.

Of values and virtue

The view from the main window of my workroom is filled by an old magnolia that was growing in the garden long before I arrived. Every now and then, with seemingly random frequency, a large saucer-shaped and creamy white flower appears, scenting the air and distracting me with its quality of ethereal resilience. The flowers are sumptuously beautiful, but short-lived, soon browning at the edges and withering back to nothingness. An image to inspire sadness? Perhaps. But since I know from past experience that another flower will almost certainly appear, it might also be an expression of hope. Or a sense of salvation. Or am I merely flirting with pathetic fallacy?

We use words to ascribe values, often without pausing to think about the process. Words like love or freedom are hounded into threadbare irrelevance by having to justify all manner of whimsical – and often dangerous – nonsense. Some time ago, an ABC radio instant guru on Iraq mentioned the 'rules of war' as if this piece of fatuous Marine-speak was of moral value. War is politically sanctioned barbarity, and to perpetuate the myth that it operates under a set of enforceable rules is to spit in the eye of sanity. Our prime minister at the time talked of war in the same breath as 'Australian values', by which he appeared to mean a laconic recognition of tolerance (although John Howard's values tended to be opportunistic and could change according to circumstance). Given the way his government treated asylum seekers, the merest nod towards tolerance was a breathtaking hypocrisy. His words and values on terrorism and Iraq were cause for even greater concern. If – as he claimed – we didn't go war to find weapons of mass destruction, and terrorism was already a global reality, precisely why did we go to war? If it was to rid the world of a dangerous regime, we should – using the same criteria – have considered invading at least half a dozen other countries, including America, since arguably its imperial arrogance over the past fifty years has done more than most to prevent international harmony. And what of John Howard's ludicrous claim that supporting America made no difference to our risk of becoming a terrorist target?

It is palpably obvious, except to idiots and liars, that the war on Iraq made the world (including our piece of it) much more dangerous. Not only has it recruited additional terrorists, it has encouraged previously opposed fundamentalist groups to pool their hatred of the West in general and America in particular. In my opinion, the West's response to terrorism has been wrong, every step of the way, since 11 September 2001 and, far from solving existing problems, has created many more; most of them of even greater danger and complexity. I repeat now what I said then, as the dust settled on what remained of the twin towers: when someone hates you enough to do what they did, it makes sense to consider why the hatred exists before punching in the smart bomb target codes. The moment George Dubya declared, with the empty boast of a schoolyard bully, 'We are good, they are evil,' he locked the gates against any chance of demonstrating the West's assumption of goodness, and set us all – without sensible consultation – on a downward spiral into an-eye-for-an-eye expression of violence and madness.

But it's not just fundamentalism or military imperialism where our so-called values have been losing the plot. Recently, a *Canberra Times* front-page photo spread garnished the story about Nicole Kidman having received more than twenty-five million dollars for a single year of looking good, and remembering a few lines of make-believe drama script every now and then. There are so many different ways of going bonkers in this mad, bad and dangerous world that I hesitate to mention the one about trying to work out how such an extravagant payment might be justified. If Nicole had discovered a cure for cancer, or succeeded in getting the Palestinians and Jews to stop killing each other, her vast reward might have meant something. In the context of third-world poverty, starving children, and our religious myths about equality and love, it made about as much moral sense as invading Iraq, or the claim that suicide bombers have no other choice. And goes a considerable way to explaining why the world remains such a screwed-up place.

I've just paused to admire the magnolia again. And noticed there are no white flowers. None. I could have sworn there was at least one in place at the start of this essay. Maybe they only appear at certain times of the year, and I imagined a randomly spread display? Maybe I saw what I expected to see. Maybe I'm going bonkers.

In truth, I suspect we're all blundering around in the dark whistling, but not particularly well disposed towards admitting it. Because, to do so, would run the risk of bringing the entire puffed-up edifice of human species self-importance down around our ears. The values John Howard drove need a new set of ethical brake pads before we all finish up in a ditch. But given Honest John's ability to find virtue in a moral wasteland, he'd probably come up smelling of magnolias. Even if they weren't there.

Of ethos and education

Civilisation is defined by the ethos and education of its community, and the means by which social justice is achieved. Perhaps the UN should consider appointing a Council of Wise Elders, who would annually assess every nation in terms of ethos, education, health, and social justice, to arrive at a CQ (civilisation quotient) which might be used to coerce recalcitrants into lifting their game. A CQ rating would have no bearing on economic factors (which are already well surveyed) because of how they often eschew true reflections of social justice. For example, John Howard was sufficiently proud of his balance sheets to see them as being the ultimate arbiter of what could or couldn't be done, but in humanitarian terms his government would have struggled to score a CQ rating (on a scale of one to ten) of much more than three. On a wider canvas, if we – as a human species – in the past century could have somehow collectively produced at least one generation of children who had been wanted and loved, the world would be a much more amenable place.

When a child is abused or neglected, it becomes a blue-chip investment in future social pain. We wring our hands over crime rates, youth suicide, drugs and the disintegration of human community, but lack the collective will to engage ideas that might make a difference. This is probably because they're likely to seem confronting, but a civilised society should be able to consider lateral thinking without feeling threatened. Most of us would agree that our system of education is in need of reinvention. Many of our important life skills, such as those to do with relationship behaviour, tolerance and social justice, are neglected, even ignored, while traditionally academic subjects are still force-fed, and quickly forgotten. Increasingly, research is suggesting that a caring and playfully stimulating environment during childhood is a major key to adult stability.

With this is mind, here's a lateral idea about changing the ethos of education. At least one parent (of either gender) should be encouraged – and, if need be, funded – to actively care for children in the first nine years following birth. During this time, there would be no formal education, other than development of reading, writing and numeracy skills as part of family or community story telling and games. Children would be allowed the time to celebrate childhood, through creative use of the imagination, interaction with each other and appropriately relevant adults. On their tenth birthday, these children would enter a formal period of education, lasting at least eight years and including many of the practical living skills hitherto assumed to be acquired by osmosis (probably behind the bike shed) together with classes designed to increase a social awareness of how economics, politics, sexuality and prejudice really work, at a global as well as local level. After this, those inclined by personality and intellect towards university study likely to provide a usefully humanitarian life skill would be encouraged to take up such study, without any regard for economic considerations.

I have little doubt that, after a generation or two of such a system, many of the serious social problems we wrestle with today would have atrophied into insignificance, although finding the political leaders willing to engage such a proposition is entirely another matter.

However, it's not merely the ethos of education that begs examination, it's the day-to-day relevance of learning. Knowledge comes but wisdom lingers, said the poet, and an educated fool can be more bother than a philistine. For example, you shouldn't need a degree in sociology to realise that a society where a minority of the population owns and controls a majority of the wealth is always going to be troubled, and yet we actively encourage such a system. Similarly, it's illogical to have spent the past few hundred years modernising industry so that it functions under the efforts of fewer people, but fail to grasp (or maybe deliberately ignore) the fact that, unless we're prepared to adequately compensate the dispossessed, a genuine sense of community will remain out of reach.

A truly civilised society would educate people to share available resources, and reassess the Protestant work ethic (which helps stigmatise unemployment) in order to live more comfortably with leisure. We've struggled to the point of slavery and death to achieve freedom from many things, including work, and maybe we should consider enjoying some distraction by use of creativity totally unrelated to the concept of working for money.

However, all this presupposes leadership of sufficient imagination to realise that economic theory is not (and never should be) the final argument. Decency, tolerance and compassion are abstractions; they can't be number-crunched onto balance sheets, but remain, nevertheless, poignant shadows of a better world. I've always considered the essence of democracy to be a reconciliation between self-interest and community interest, and it's worth remembering that community interest also serves self-interest, but self-interest only serves itself.

Perhaps the most serious problem we all share as human beings at the moment is that of accepting ourselves as we are, rather than as we think we are. John Ralston Saul, in *The Unconscious Civilisation*, listed desirable human qualities as 'commonsense, creativity or imagination, ethics (not morality), intuition or instinct, memory and, finally, reason.' Which is probably a good place to rest.

Of media and morality

The difference between journalism and literature, Oscar Wilde once loftily proclaimed, is that no one reads literature and journalism is unreadable. The truth, I suspect, is that most people skim both and, while it probably does little harm to claim to have read James Joyce's *Ulysses* by flipping the pages, doing something similar with the media's coverage of current political reality might explain how John Howard and George W. Bush both managed to escape electoral retribution.

The way in which we receive information related to making sensible democratic choices arguably constitutes one of the most important debates of our increasingly immoral age. An open and fair-minded media, fearlessly reporting on day-to-day performances of elected politicians, as well as decisions made by corporate leaders affecting ordinary lives, is widely considered achievable, if not already in place. The fact that both the concluding parts of this proposition are demonstrably false (the second part laughably so) doesn't stop leaders trotting them out whenever the circumstances suit. Of course, they know very well, as does anyone else who cares to look closely and honestly at how our system is financially and socially framed, that the reality is much more shop-soiled.

Basically, this merely reflects the nature of a materialist society; after all, the ethos of capitalism is hardly likely to report its activities in a manner inclined to diminish profit. In much the same way, politicians are always likely to place a positive spin on stories they feel might work against them. And we all tend to possess a moral blind spot when it comes to noticing the prejudicial nature of our own actions. One of the most untouchable aspects of racism, for example, is the resolutely stubborn way it resists recognising itself. As any good counsellor knows, the best way to attack a problem is to first accept that the problem exists.

I believe there's a problem with the way the media failed to report the morality of a federal government that was allowed to dismiss a significant body of national and international critical evidence, then go on to win the 2004 election which common sense and decency suggested it should have lost. Of course, this was seen by the winners as the whingeing refrain of a loser, but that's precisely my point: how easily perceptions of right- and left-wing politics can wilfully misconstrue the process of democracy.

Personally, I prefer to talk in terms of what might be right or wrong, good or bad, or the incremental steps of developing genuine social justice, rather than enter the cul-de-sac of political ideology. But this is the hand I've been dealt, so let's cut to the chase, and reveal the nub of ideological tension between right- and left-wing positions. It's money. Simply that. In terms of wants versus needs. The right fears the left will steal its money, and the left assumes the right already has.

Economically rationalist states, like Australia, are increasingly divided between people with money and little time, and people with time and little money. Unless adjusted by appropriate equal opportunity legislation, this gap between rich and poor will continue to grow. Just as there will never be peace without justice, as Booker prize-winning novelist, Arundhati Roy, recently reminded us, there will never be justice without equality. And this has nothing to do with left-wing ideology; it's to do with finding the imagination to somehow make sure people are not disadvantaged by actions outside their own responsibility. In other words, there's an important moral distinction between wasting opportunities and not being given a chance to use them.

In a moral sense, deliberate misconstruction of the truth is worse than a lie. John Howard liked to split hairs on what did or didn't constitute honesty, and yet it should have been obvious to anyone lacking the shock-jock prejudice of Alan Jones that the Howard government deliberately misconstrued the truth regarding many issues, notably the war on Iraq, and its disgraceful treatment of asylum seekers. The fact that (with a few honourable exceptions) these matters were not reported in a way in which even the most disengaged voter might have noticed the smell, morally condemns the media.

Of culture and control

'When I hear the word culture,' Hermann Goering is supposed to have commented, during the doomed control of his führer's thousand-year Reich, 'I reach for my revolver.' No doubt, he was thinking of the kind of 'intellectual elite' that insisted on disturbing John Howard's eleven-year tyranny of ignorance; far easier to rule a bunch of semi-comatose halfwits than a rabble of educated 'bleeding hearts' who might just care about the injustice being thrust on people other than themselves.

Let's define our terms: 'culture' is an expression of collective meaning, and 'control' a downwardly exerted social force made from positions of power, wealth or charisma – particularly the first two. I have no doubt that our utterly fatuous faith in economic growth has vandalised Western culture to the point where you're likely to be seen as part of a dangerously intellectual elite if you prefer to flick through a gardening magazine rather than watch reality TV. We are living in the Age of Banality. And those in control know very well how this works in their favour. Bigotry, prejudice and intolerance occur because people are simply too lazy, dumb or disconnected to separate truth from the myth. And let's define a myth by saying it is mostly a lie behaving as if it were the truth. The Howard government was a consummate myth. The so-called coalition of the willing was a mega-myth. The self-justifying machinations of Bush, Blair and Howard would constitute a useful PhD thesis for any student of psychology. As would the Howard government's unrelentingly cruel mismanagement of asylum seekers. The trouble is, in an Age of Banality, palpable injustice becomes reduced to the irritating background buzz of a single mosquito on a balmy summer night.

Often, at three in the morning, when I can't sleep, and have to face the hour Napoleon is supposed to have described as that requiring the greatest degree of courage to look squarely in the eye, my hand wanders over my bedside bookshelves, usually settling on a volume of essays from a different age. George Orwell, Bertrand Russell or George Bernard Shaw. Let's take a snippet at random from each, starting with Orwell:

> I never read the proclamations of generals before battle, the speeches of fuhrers and prime ministers, the solidarity songs of public schools and left-wing political parties, national anthems, Temperance tracts, papal encyclicals and sermons against gambling and contraception, without seeming to hear in the background a chorus of raspberries from all the millions of common men to whom these high sentiments make no appeal.

Then Bertrand Russell:

> Some kind of philosophy is a necessity to all but the most thoughtless, and in the absence of knowledge it is almost sure to be a silly philosophy. The result of this is that the human race becomes divided into rival groups of fanatics, each group firmly persuaded that its own brand of nonsense is sacred truth, while the other side's is damnable heresy… Dogmatism is an enemy to peace, and an insuperable barrier to democracy.

And finally the indefatigable GBS:

> Once and for all, we are not born free; and we never can be free. When all the human tyrants are slain or deposed there will still be the supreme tyrant that can never be slain or deposed, and that tyrant is Nature.

It would seem that, despite our technology, we have failed to achieve a great deal of progress in terms of human civilisation, whatever that process might involve. Simply behaving decently to each other would seem like a good start. Hell's teeth! Australia had children locked away who spent their entire lives behind razor wire! And politicians, on both sides of a barely audible, and risibly inadequate, asylum seeker debate, stood around splitting hairs about who was most responsible. A child who has known no other environment than a prison sponsored by a government that was democratically elected by a supposedly tolerant society is an insult to the intelligence of a moron. And yet I know several people who voted for the Howard government who are clearly not morons. Neither are they psychopaths. For the most part, they are decent people, who love their families, don't kick their dogs, and appear to behave in a law-abiding fashion. How then, do we account for such an obvious inconsistency? By understanding how culture (that is, collective meaning) can be controlled through the cynical generation of fear and prejudice, and how self-interest is deliberately – and fatally – linked to the distracting greed of never-ending economic growth.

Meaning is not fixed: it is flexible, and can be construed to fit the permutations of a controlling power. And measured to meet the expectations of those being controlled by that power. Think about it.

Of lethargy and the left

There were times during the turbulent twentieth century when fascism flourished and communism seemed likely to prevail against the odds. Maybe some of the old Bolshevik idealism lingers on in socialism, like the sad ghost of revolutions past, but terrorism has become the new 'evil empire', and the only other political ism still thriving in the twenty-first century is capitalism, the one championed by the Right and driven by self-interest and greed, which the Left famously dismissed as being near death during the latter part of the nineteenth century.

It's diverting to speculate – from the depths of a politically induced existential depression over the Howard government's apparent immunity from rage or reason (like some new strain of attack-resistant virus) – what Karl Marx would have made of how thoroughly his prediction about capitalism seems to have failed. I've never been much more than an emotional Marxist, regarding most economic theory to be as incomprehensible (and therefore as socially irrelevant) as postmodern poetry, but still see the Left as our best chance of achieving anything remotely close to a civilisation based on genuine social justice. It therefore follows that I dismiss with contempt the Right's tedious contention that the Left is merely a refuge for ineffectual bleeding hearts, lacking the guts to face the reality of free-market forces, or the fuzzily fundamental fugues of economic rationalism.

Maybe we should ask ourselves what we really mean by categorising people as coming from the Left or Right. Do these labels serve any useful purpose, other than shoring up a few nebulous political stereotypes? In eighteenth-century France, the National Assembly placed moderates in the centre, democrats and extremists on the left, and reactionaries on the right, thus establishing a loosely based classification system which has survived into the twenty-first century. Nowadays, both sides regard the other with equal disdain, although there seems to be a wary consensus that the Left focuses more on issues, and the Right on outcomes, with each claiming moral superiority.

I remember being amused, and a trifle miffed when Michael Duffy, the ABC's newly engaged 'right-wing Phillip Adams' (surely an oxymoron?), was interviewed on ABC FM by Margaret Throsby. Responding to a question as to when, why and how he had achieved his lauded right-wing status, he replied along the lines that he had started from a left-wing student perspective, but as he grew older (and by implication, wiser) he'd turned inevitably towards the Right. I was astonished. The older I get (leaving aside any considerations of wisdom), the more the Left satisfies my perception of what constitutes a reasonable response to this wicked old world. And this belief, I hasten to add, is based on humanitarian, rather than economic, grounds. As I have argued many times before, decency, tolerance and truth are abstract values. They can't be number-crunched onto balance sheets, or loaded into weapons carriers. But they play a vital role in our human development and survival. Of this, I am certain.

Many pundits argued that the ALP lost federal elections because it didn't match the government on economic management. Codswallop! What about management of health, education and social justice? I'm not saying governments should spend recklessly – obviously, a basic premise of any form of legislative control should be to recognise economic responsibility – but I think the ALP would have stood a better chance if it had offered voters a clear alternative by attempting to rediscover the values of its True Believers: the people who are likely to consider that ethics are more important than balance sheets; that traumatised families don't belong behind razor wire; and that a pre-emptive war makes as much sense as clobbering a derelict in a dark alley just to make sure he doesn't clobber you first. We all do well to remember that when someone hates you enough to kill themselves in an effort to kill you, it might be useful to try to understand why that hatred exists before invading a regime wrongly accused of supporting them.

And since I'm building up a head of steam, let me squeeze in a couple of subsidiary concerns about language and logic in the aftermath of that terrible day in September 2001. Our cultural practice is to place the day before the month and say 11th of September not September 11. Therefore, in an English-speaking environment, the day fundamentalism became a global threat should be remembered as 11/9 rather than 9/11. And what's all this presidential tosh about waging a 'war on terror'? How, exactly, can war be waged on an abstract noun? By throwing copies of *Roget's Thesaurus* at it, perhaps?

I'm glad I got that off my chest, but what about the Left, I hear you cry. Does it still possess contemporary relevance? Of course it does. But in order to find it, we must first defeat the dreadful lethargy that disengaged the electorate under the relentlessly selfish regime of Dubya's deputy sheriff. And that involves thinking about things that are difficult and not always likely to work towards immediate personal gain. The old adage about getting the government we deserve is true.

Of parable and power

'A little learning,' wrote Alexander Pope in his worthy *Essay on Criticism*, 'is a dangerous thing, drink deep, or taste not the Pierian spring'. A poetic reference to Piera, an area of Thessaly in Ancient Greece, supposedly the place where the Divine benefit of a Muse was first noticed. 'Knowledge comes,' Tennyson added, over a hundred years later, 'but wisdom lingers.'

Both observations are true. Failure to see the big picture can be misleading, and education doesn't always bring enlightenment. Ignorance might be bliss, and is best kept apart from power, but it seldom becomes as dangerous as half-baked knowledge. As we contemplate the federal government's security paranoia, we do well to remind ourselves that few people – on either side of the global terrorism fence – are as evil or as sacrosanct as we like to suppose. Many are simply thrashing around trying to find answers to questions they haven't fully understood, and making frequently foolish assumptions as a result. Whether it's a pathetic parable of good versus evil, or a leadership dispute at the local croquet club, we should never underestimate the distorting power of a partially formed view.

Our system of parliamentary democracy is being diminished by dangerous levels of disengagement. A bitterly disappointed Mark Latham gave a lecture at Melbourne University offering ten reasons for avoiding election as a politician, including public apathy, loss of privacy, negative impact on family, and the arrogant incompetence of the media. How much of this was an expression of frustration over his own political demise is anyone's guess, but reflects enough public disenchantment to worry those of us who believe – as I do – that if we can't reach a halfway decent society through the democratic choice of suitably qualified politicians, we're not going to get there at all. Mark Latham wound up his argument with these words:

> If you are a young, idealistic person, don't get involved in organised politics. Contribute to your community, your neighbourhood, your immediate circle of trust and support. This is the best way forward for a better society.

I agree with the second sentence of that statement. The well-spring of any healthy society is a sense of community trust and support. However, unless abstract values like these are somehow granted visible legality through government legislation, they fall easy prey to the philistines, whose aspirations are more likely based on self-interest and urban mythology than finding socially equitable solutions.

Unfortunately, it's becoming increasingly difficult to argue against the notion that politicians are primarily motivated by power. Bob Hawke's 1980s headline-grabbing media bite about no child living in poverty by 1990 is a case in point. Hawke must have known the phrase would come back to haunt him, but hunger for short-term power was enough to push this possibility aside. My disappointment with Kim Beazley went even deeper, although in mitigation I believe his political luck was lousy (consider the timing of Tampa and the Towers) and by attempting to play the bipartisan card (however well-intentioned) he alienated Labor's heartland. However, I suspect Kim Beazley was more than the sum of his disappointing parts, and agree with Neal Blewett's perceptive comment about him being the sort of politician likely to have performed better in power than in opposition.

A good leader knows when to soft-pedal, and John Howard's risible anti-terrorism posture reminded me of the D.H. Lawrence parable about a society that tried so hard to protect itself from fear that it produced the very fear it was trying to avoid. In such an environment, words like tragedy, freedom and truth are terminally diminished by extravagant use, but the scenario facing us now – as fundamentalism squares off against arrogance – is a tragedy in excess of anything the ancient Greeks might have imagined. Splinters of this great tragedy are being driven deep into the heart of twenty-first century politics. A good leader would try to heal these wounds rather than seek to exploit them.

Not so long ago in the story of our world, we identified consciousness as being the single defining difference between us and other living species. The cross we must bear is our wretched awareness of ourselves as human beings, from whose context we sometimes pause to consider our condition under the tenuously abstracted light of ethics and morality. Sadly, the arrogance of easily assumed superiority encourages us to make judgements – largely based on religious myth – about what we consider to be good or evil. If they exist as separate entities, which I very much doubt, good and evil are merely aspects of each other, with relative values indelibly referenced to cultural, spiritual or political points of view. After all, who has any right to say – above and beyond the rare occurrence of obvious and indisputable evidence – that one belief system is better or worse than another? We collectively inhabit a speck of cosmic dust in a vast and apparently otherwise unoccupied universe. Surely it is wasteful nonsense to fatally quarrel over how we choose to live on fragments of that speck of dust? Surely it makes much more sense to try to share what we agree to call life? However we wish to explain it. However we choose to worship it. And ultimately, however we profess to judge it.

Of community and care

A sense of community, where people care for each other and generally trust their elected leaders, forms the bedrock of any halfway decent society. Unfortunately, it's a paradox of human nature to want government without being governed. But anarchy doesn't work and few people trust politicians. Perhaps because some of them (like Peter Reith during the 1999 referendum campaign to see if Australia wanted to become a republic) are not above the astonishingly cynical act of fomenting that distrust for their own ends. Which soon becomes the Cretan liar paradox: how do I know politicians are untrustworthy? Because a politician told me so.

Obviously, a democracy burdened by such robust levels of cynicism and disengagement is in poor health, perhaps terminally so, but finding a cure is never going to be easy. Nor is it likely to be quick. Expecting significant social change to happen overnight is as unrealistic as telling someone to be spontaneous – or happy. These things happen obliquely, almost always as a result of something else, and usually take time.

So, what is this mysterious force – this something else – that might persuade a rediscovery of ourselves as conscious and caring human beings, willing to engage with the participation imperative of democracy? A collective sense of meaning might help, preferably positive, but unlikely to plummet into the paranoid depths of fundamentalism or gratuitous flag-waving. Here in Australia, for example, a decade of me-first materialism, with its blind devotion to economic growth, has produced a culture of self-centred banality, where abstractions such as tolerance, trust and compassion are likely to be scorned as weakness, and reduced to fluffy embarrassments, like crying at sentimental films, or feeling sorry for the handicapped. Oh yes, we can still manage an occasionally generous whip-round when some of our third-world neighbours get wiped out by a tsunami, but it takes a bureaucratic balls-up of diabolical dimension to expose our inhumane treatment of traumatised refugees.

One issue providing a telling illustration of how we lack the care that might define a decent community is the way we handle mental health. A disgraceful proportion of our prison population is increasingly comprised of people who are mentally ill and indigent rather than criminally culpable and wicked. Our prisons are stealthily becoming de facto psychiatric wards, presumably because it's easier to slam and bolt the door on dysfunctional behaviour rather than try to find the kind of care that might help retrieve an acceptable community level of functionality.

Take depression as an example of an increasingly common, but dangerously misunderstood, mental illness. A state premier and a fading football star made brief news splashes when the former resigned and the latter took his own life as a means of coping with the unimaginable torment of clinical depression. We paused, made a few collectively sympathetic noises, and went back to what we had been doing before. Meanwhile, the affliction of clinical depression extends its sinister reach.

For a sufferer, being given a chance to talk about your depression is one of the most powerfully healing elements of recovery. Sadly, unless you're a celebrity (and therefore universally lauded for having the courage to speak), you're likely to encounter increasing hostility and rejection to your admission of mental suffering. A key reason relates to invisibility. Someone in the potentially fatal grip of full-on depression can seem much the same as anyone else. Often, they can appear to cope with the daily requirements of life much the same as anyone else (although usually at a high price). Mental illness is mostly subjective. A physical handicap can be quantified and assessed: a bone is broken, an organ dysfunctions, or a series of cells begin to mutate, but psychological handicap has no readily identifiable parameters. Largely, it's down to someone's point of view; a subjective interpretation of how far individual behaviour

31

has deviated from an acceptable norm. And since 'normal' is itself a subjective perception, an accurate or meaningful definition of what is or isn't mental illness becomes hit or miss. Which works against recovery, and inevitably makes things worse for the sufferer, rather than better.

Community outcomes are inclined to be more inclusive, further-reaching and closer to concepts of humanity than institutional ones. There are no real reasons – other than stupidity, bloody-minded ignorance and ego-driven greed – why we, as a human species, shouldn't accept our collective lot and get on with living together in a manner that provides the greatest possible good for everyone. The fact that this obvious position appears unobtainable suggests that unless we can somehow find political leadership that cares more for humanity than it does for itself we are not long for this world.

Of man and mammon

In the fourth century, Saint Augustine observed that we were corrupt and helpless sinners. Little has changed. As a human species, we seem unable to resist corruption. Is this an irredeemable flaw? Augustine's theory was that we were born this way in order to allow us the chance of choosing a life of atonement; but being an unbeliever, I'm of the view that the reason has more to do with the politics of self-interest, and the ease with which we become seduced by vanity and greed. In an essay titled 'The Depreciated Legacy of Cervantes', Milan Kundera makes this perceptive comment:

> Man desires a world where good and evil can be clearly distinguished, for he has an innate and irrepressible desire to judge before he understands.

Indeed! If only we could learn to understand more and judge less.

How easily the personal becomes the political. Conflicting ideologies of capitalism and socialism are constituted in a manner substantially influenced by ego, and this has corrupted both systems to a point requiring the complicity of leaders and followers alike in order for the process to work. And when you factor in the obscenely huge cost of our futile struggle to maintain law and order (at an international as well as national level) – in other words, the seemingly endless amounts of time and money we must provide for defence and police systems in order to fund what is really a pathetically failed attempt to force people to behave decently to each other – you begin to realise how far we remain from the mythical status of civilisation, and what a hopeless bunch of crooks and cretins our ideological vanity has produced.

A neglected key that might unlock the human enigma involves reconciling the difference between what we feel and what we think, and understanding how these reactions – the emotional and the intellectual – can argue with each other to the detriment of both. The reconciliation process begins with imagination, and imagination begins by allowing it to begin. By asking 'what if?' – and not being prejudiced or intimidated by possible answers. For example, a well-educated and healthy society, the costs of which are funded by public revenue, should be the basic entry point for any civilisation, and yet the bean counters quibble, saying we can't afford such a proposition. And the chief reason we can't afford it is because of the colossal expenditure mentioned above, concerned with constantly preparing for (and occasionally prosecuting) war, and simply trying to make sure the population obeys an increasing number of laws.

Well, how about this for a 'what if' hypothetical? Wouldn't an educated and healthy community (local or global) be less inclined to cheat, steal or kill in order to assuage real or imagined injustice? In other words, spending money on improving the health, education and self-esteem of the disadvantaged (preferably by methods other than international aid, charity or welfare payments, all of which are too easily corrupted) would eventually mean a lot less would need to be spent on law enforcement, prisons and war. Emotionally, I would suggest, this is an idea of such common sense to offer far-reaching social progress, but intellectually, of course, it will be seen as dangerously naïve. The gap between how we feel and think about complex and socially sensitive issues frequently require creative reconciliation. And that's where we are being short-changed by the bankrupt imaginations of our elected representatives.

A positive-feel response to a hypothetical question about public funding for health and education is likely to invoke a negative-thought reaction largely because it collides with the human propensity for taking what we have for granted – almost as if it were the consequence of some divine right, rather than merely the result of a series of fortuitous social, geographic and climatic circumstances.

To place ourselves in a realistic historical and global context requires imagination. For example, against the vast span of time since we slouched out of Africa, our recent century of relative comfort represents the blink of an eyelid. And even this must be placed against the sociological reality of the immensely uneven (and palpably unjust) disparity in the distribution of human resources and wealth. Far too easily we forget that our Western developed lifestyle is the global exception rather than the rule, and that the vast majority of the world's population live substantially lesser lives.

But probably the most costly failure of imagination has to do with war. The war on Iraq was motivated by revenge, justified by a lie and perpetuated by arrogance. Any war is a grotesque waste of lives, time and money, but the war on Iraq (and its consequent, and inanely labelled, 'war on terror') was also a culpably stupid waste of the lives, time and money we should have been deploying on solving the potentially fatal global threat of climate change. The hatred generated by Western arrogance during the second half of the twentieth century has probably already done enough to ensure that the twenty-first century will be our last. If it hasn't, then global warming will take care of whatever is left. And this doomsday scenario has arisen because we've neglected imagination, and predicated ideology on the dimensions of Mammon rather than Man.

Of ego and economics

I've coined a new term – post-pragmatic – for our ego-driven and economically rationalist age to explain the world-weary hopelessness that says, in effect, everything is beyond redemption, and we may as well accept the morally bankrupt notion that ends justify means, and keep our fingers collectively crossed. Should anyone doubt this, they have only to glance at widespread corporate corruption and so-called 'pre-emptive' war.

Terrorism has replaced communism as a focus for the developed world's fear and loathing in the twenty-first century. In a famously doomed attempt to stop the First World War, the concluding sentence of a resolution taken at the Second International in Basle proclaimed,

> Let the capitalist world of exploitation and mass murder be confronted by the proletarian world of peace and international brotherhood.

In all the countless words of commentary concerning the Iraq war, no one (as far as I am aware) has explored, far less mentioned, the classical irony of the region having been part of what was once known as Mesopotamia and considered a cradle of civilisation pre-dating the Greeks. I often wonder – usually at three o'clock in the morning – whether there is more to admire than despise in our confused and convoluted progress from the swamp to the stars. The war on Iraq was a great nonsense, and attempting to impose Western democracy at the point of a gun on what's left of its population an even greater nonsense. But having coined the term post-pragmatic, I am at least able to frame these examples of human futility in a more or less amenable context.

Many people assume that capitalism won its twentieth-century struggle with communism, but this is predominantly based on myth; communism collapsed of its own accord, largely through internal corruption and unbridled ego, and although these aspects were – and still are – also crucially part of capitalism, they're more easily concealed by a system that operates inside a moral paradox. For example, I've always been amused, and occasionally bemused, by the way staunch capitalists are likely to be God-fearing Christians, since I have little doubt – based on what I understand of His teachings – that Christ would be a socialist if given the choice in today's world.

However, as a left-leaning unbeliever, I take the view that religion is wish-fulfilling myth; little more than a troublesome legacy from prehistoric superstition, and it's time we moved on. I also believe that neo-conservative Christian arrogance is as much to blame for contemporary global conflict as Islamic fundamentalism. And when you overlay this spiral of hate with the greed and corruption of freebooting capitalism, you begin to get some idea of the sheer implacability of our sorry state. Sadly, I must confess that my slant on socialism is more emotional than intellectual. I come from a large family, in which my siblings nicknamed me 'the Duke', and, it's true, I've always been drawn to 'nice things' – wine, music and comfortable quarters – as a romanticised means of getting through life with the least possible pain. I have no quarrel with anyone acquiring a larger slice of the cake, as long as they have done so by merit, and I'm prepared to live in a capitalist environment, even though I have little interest in taking part. But I'm passionate about social justice, and despise the holier-than-thou Christian capitalists, who celebrate opportunistic greed from Monday to Saturday, and the tolerant ministrations of their church on Sunday.

Despite some obviously serious flaws, capitalism continues to flourish, probably because of its proud claim that everyone can win. Maybe they can, but certainly not all at the same time (which would mean defeating poverty), because this would destroy a system with a vested interest in maintaining the gap between rich and poor. Successful capitalism depends on human gullibility, and every bean-counter knows that the best way to make sure the rich stay rich is to make sure the poor stay poor. There's also an arrogant assumption that everyone wants to play the game (or knows how to), and those who don't or can't (for whatever reason) are penalised. Profit doesn't exist in a vacuum. One man's dividend is another man's debit. Capitalism is essentially about making money from the arbitrarily assessed value of other money (capital), which is a vacuous process since it has no objectively intrinsic worth. Even if the other money is real. Writing in his 1997 book *The Unconscious Civilisation*, the Canadian public intellectual John Ralston Saul observed,

> Every day, currency traders move a trillion dollars around the world. This would seem to suggest that a lot of money is available. And that if a very small part of it were paid in taxes most of our public financing problems would be solved. There are, unfortunately, two impediments: this money is not available for taxation. And more importantly, it doesn't really exist.

Which would seem to suggest that capitalism works largely by illusion, with the process being generated by smoke and mirrors, controlled by ego, and consumed by credit. No wonder it occasionally collapses like a pack of cards.

Economic theory is mysterious and inaccessible, allowing kaleidoscopic interpretation, from the academic to the arcane, although personally, I seldom feel the need to dig much deeper than Mr Micawber's splendid advice: 'Annual income twenty pounds, annual expenditure nineteen pounds, nineteen and sixpence, result happiness. Annual income twenty pounds, annual expenditure twenty pounds, nought and sixpence, result misery.'

Ego and economics have always had a depressing tendency to grant mediocrity more power than it deserves, but democracy remains the best system of government we have managed to produce. At the last count we (as a human species) had invented around 6,000 languages, but still haven't found a way to speak to each other that might militate against prejudice, poverty and war. And you don't need to be a cynic to see this as evidence of how these things remain useful to the way we choose to constitute reality. A redemptive creed for the third millennium might beneficially include an attempt to bridge the gap between what we are, and what we think we are. I'll conclude with that speculative thought…

Of fear and favour

I must warn you, dear reader (if in fact you exist, for I've long suspected I'm writing in a vacuum, ignored by everyone, except Ragsie, my best mate's border collie) that these words are coming to you from a bleak landscape. Because I'm on the cusp of giving up the ghost, whatever that means – let's just say I'm in danger of being silenced by an increasing conviction that the human species doesn't deserve to survive. And this is a tough pill to swallow, since I have several grandchildren I love very much who can't be blamed for the dangerously chaotic mess they will inherit. John Howard washed his hands on Kyoto with the self-righteously flawed logic of a truant schoolboy who rejects the classroom while claiming to respect the education system. I'm certainly no betting man, but the apocalypse appears to be showing shorter odds than our survival at the moment. In this grim scenario, surely we should be doing whatever we can to protect the next generation, regardless of economic consequence?

At least climate change is managing to hook some public attention; reflected by a well-attended sustainable future forum in Bermagui, on the far south coast of NSW. Organised by the indefatigable Laurel Lloyd-Jones, the speakers included the passionate anti-nuclear campaigner, Doctor Helen Caldicott,; Doctor Matthew Nott, an orthopedic surgeon, who hit the climate change debate running with a profoundly sensible cause in Clean Energy for Eternity (check the website www.cleanenergyforeternity.net); the seductively intelligent Suzanne Foulkes, from the Friends of Five Forests organisation; the irrepressible Pat Thompson, a long-term and well-loved local, with an international jazz-singing reputation that makes light of her eighty-something years; Chris Allen, whose eco-neighbourhood development project near Bega is attracting notice; and Dean Turner, from the Crossing Land Education Centre, committed to helping young people in a fourteen to twenty-five target age group learn how to live sustainably.

Surprisingly (for me, at least) the mood was one of optimism rather than despair. Climate change poses a potential human catastrophe, but it also provides an opportunity for the kind of collective smart thinking that might substantially benefit civilisation. After all, I guess if we can find the wherewithal to survive together, we have shown each other that we can live together. A solution for climate change is eminently achievable, providing we can all engage with the lifestyle modifications required to stop poisoning the planet. And this is where my instinctive pessimism becomes turbo-charged. Because taking action at a local level, by joining community groups interested in energy conservation, self-sustainability, and curbing consumerism, is one thing; placing this mindset in a global context is a problem of an entirely different dimension. For example, even if we manage to install solar energy systems, switch off unwanted light bulbs, calibrate our water use and eventually acknowledge the lunacy of destroying our forests, terrorism and war will still be sowing their seeds of hatred, whose bitter harvest will be reaped by people increasingly resistant to working together on anything, except killing each other.

Fear has become an instrument of political strategy in the highly combustible hot air that drives the war on global terrorism, with our side's favour being bestowed on those who close ranks behind the morally bankrupt notion that right-wing Christian arrogance and neo-conservative 'values' represent the only way out of a dangerously complex labyrinth of hatred and violence. Sadly, our aggressively adversarial parliament is concerned more with self-righteous and rhetorical argument than with truth, diminishing the chance of ever reaching the sort of powerfully non-partisan stance required to achieve a degree of international cooperation that might deflect the additionally lethal threat of climate change.

We know what is causing our planet to overheat. We know what needs to be done to fix it. And we also know that it can be fixed. But only if we all take part. Which means movers and shakers on both sides of the depressingly self-serving and fatuously named 'war on terror' must be somehow persuaded that if they can't sublimate their present hatred into future care, there will be no winners. Just losers. Followed by the awfully long silence of a dead planet; haunted by the cooling stones and bones of an amazing, but tragically unfulfilled, human species.

Of shoes and ships

'The time has come,' the Walrus said,
'To talk of many things:
Of shoes and ships – and sealing wax –
Of cabbages and kings –
And why the sea is boiling hot –
And whether pigs have wings.'

Lewis Carroll (1832–98)

We live on a chunk of cosmic dust, shaped like a huge tennis ball, spinning rapidly through a vacuum, and trapped inside a vast and unimaginable mystery, but somehow manage to carry on as if none of that existed; as if finding a parking spot and remembering to put the rubbish out on collection nights, were matters of elemental importance. Questions about what we are, and why we are, have occupied superstition and science for many thousands of years, and yet, on a balance of probabilities, still don't have answers; at least, not the sort we expect to find. In fact, it's the ultimate catch-22: if the fabric of our existence were simple enough for us to understand, we would be too simple to understand it.

As a child, growing up in the south of England in the aftermath of the Second World War, I knew – and presumed to understand – my immediate world with all the intimacy of love. It was – and mostly still is – an astonishingly beautiful place. Grassy downs, gently sloping towards brooding cliffs, with caves and rocky bays that might have come from the pages of a Robert Louis Stevenson adventure yarn. Wandering lanes with leafy hedgerows, where birds would nest as foxes skulked and squirrels scampered. There were daffodils and bluebells, wild and unattended, springing up in clusters of startling colour as winter thawed, and gorse bushes, whose yellow-flowered musky scent can still open a time tunnel for me as redolent as any Proustian biscuit. At the heart of this enchanted landscape was a small but mysterious wood of oaks, into which I disappeared with notebook and pencil to dream of shoes and ships and sealing wax…and one day climbing the mountain of becoming a writer.

Little wonder Stevenson's seductive line about the world being so full of wonderful things; we should all be as happy and wealthy as kings, carried such powerful appeal. Of course, I have since come to realise that what I regarded as an entire world was only a tiny fragment, protected by impressionable shyness and over-active sensitivity. It did, however, provide a valuable lesson in shaping what is now a principal theme of my writing: the way we all become prisoners of our perception. Hardly an original idea, I know, since ancient Jewish writing identified the syndrome before the birth of Christ: we don't see things as they are; we see them as we are.

When I consider the world today, seen darkly through the glass of global terrorism, environmental chaos and the context of our theme – imagination, politics and change – my childhood on the south coast of England seems a starship flight away, belonging to another galaxy rather than merely a different hemisphere. Imagination is a vital part of whatever it is that makes us human, but its role in the theatre of politics and change has yet to be fully tested, and we do well to remember that imagination, particularly when mixed with intelligence, can become a heady, even dangerous, brew. Provision must be made for the sobering influence of common sense, which, ironically, is not very common at all. We must also develop a system of politics that recognises and understands the difference between knowledge and wisdom, and how an educated fool can be more dangerous than the unlettered enthusiast. We like to believe, certainly in the light of the microchip revolution, that we are a pretty smart bunch, although I suspect the reality is somewhat different, and apart from a few obvious, but relatively isolated, examples of breakthrough ingenuity, we are (as a species) nowhere near as clever or as special as we think. The trouble is, we tend to take so many things for granted. Nowadays, most people in the First World live like kings of infinite space, sustained by silicon chip technology they barely comprehend, but as recently as two hundred years ago, the only source of light and heat was an open flame. What we need, as we slouch towards a possible twenty-first century apocalypse, is a sense of humanity and compassion, rather than the selfish, dollar-driven antics of never-ending economic growth. It is evidence of wisdom, not weakness, to change political direction in response to altered circumstances, and to ignore the present compelling need for change is either disingenuous or simply dumb.

Of truth and tribulation

Recently, from the darkness of a midnight watch, I scribbled nine words into my bedside notebook: 'we are told lies, but we learn the truth'. What prompted this stark observation? As far as I am aware, the words are my own; unless I've subconsciously cribbed them. As a constant (and eclectic) reader, it's difficult, if not impossible, to remember. Apart from newspapers and magazines, garnished by a drizzle of background data from cyberspace, I usually read several books a week, and it's becoming difficult to remember the most recent title, let alone the most recent paragraph. However, I'm careful to source my notebook quotes and, since this one has no attribution, I'll claim it as my own. If I'm wrong, no doubt *Media Watch* will expose me in due course.

We are told lies, but we learn the truth. Was I attempting a Sufi poem…or a desk-calendar aphorism? In fact, I suspect the line was triggered by a juxtaposition of two things: the first, a bundle of Australian literary magazines, given to me by a friend, which I'd stacked on the floor next to my bedside table, to dip into over a week of wakeful moments, until convinced that those responsible should be punished by being forced to listen to an endless loop of Alexander Downer's press conferences; and the second, some half-finished notes for an essay I was trying to write on the mutually exclusive properties of politics and truth.

Most of the poetry, short fiction and essays in my bedside bundle of Ozlit magazines seemed curiously remote (rather like Alexander's press conferences), with a self-serving and precious reality, unlikely to gain empathy with the everyday world. No wonder contemporary Australian literary fiction and poetry is considered such a high publishing risk. No wonder people tend to fall asleep (or off a cliff) five minutes after a politician starts talking. No wonder our culture is becoming increasingly banal, and literature losing the social relevance that might help discover leaders with the imagination and integrity to get us safely through the twenty-first century.

Perhaps, dear reader, you're not convinced of this supposed need for Australian literature to be socially relevant, rather than merely good (I suspect it's usually regarded as a yet another example of left-leaning intellectual elitism), but Australian literature from the first half of the twentieth century – in other words, this nation's formative years – was certainly socially relevant; and arguably politically so, as well. (I direct you to the work of writers such as Katherine Susannah Prichard, Xavier Herbert, Eleanor Dark, Kylie Tennant, Henry Lawson and many others, for evidence supporting this proposition.) The current crop of Ozlit talent – a few names honourably excepted; Helen Garner springs immediately to mind – generally lack the passionate social intensity of that earlier group. And this has more to do with mainstream publishing than writing; where an increasingly relentless profit motive has marginalised unknown (or little-known) writers interested in challenging the superficial imperatives of today's culture of instant gratification. The tragedy of a contemporary Proust, Joyce, or Patrick White, born to blush unseen, in a system shamelessly mortgaged to banality, is essentially part of a political dynamic willing to sacrifice imagination for economic growth.

And if I had heard John Howard complain one more time that ratifying Kyoto would damage the economy, I would have pleaded insanity and belted him over the head with the heaviest volume of Hansard I can lay my hands on. The notion that an economy is more important than the environment in which it must operate is risibly fatuous, and begs the image of an alien spaceship landing on earth, in a hundred years' time, with its crew looking round at the ruins of a barren landscape, scratching their heads and saying, 'Well, they may have killed their planet, but there is evidence to suggest that their economy was sound.'

I'm finishing this piece as the sun breaks through rain clouds on the morning of Anzac Day, with the volume turned down on the bedside radio, as it whispers stories of patriotism, flags, medals and bugled-summoned dawn service crowds in my half-attentive ear. I've never been convinced by the Anzac tradition. I acknowledge that the First World War must have been an experience of horror beyond the imagination of anyone who wasn't there, and I certainly respect the courage and sacrifice of those who were, but war is almost never justified, and invariably diminishes the humanity of both sides. There is obviously nothing wrong with remembering and mourning the loss and suffering of ancestors, but beneath the sentimentalised choreography of Anzac Day I sense the barely repressed jingoism of playground heroics, where the pride of wounded grief is nurtured into tribulation. I'm sorry, but in these dangerous days of Islamic fundamentalism versus right-wing Christian arrogance, I really think it's time the Anzac bugles started playing some different tunes.

Of governments and gods

The other evening, as is my melancholic wont, I took a solitary walk by the sea near Bermagui, on the far south coast of New South Wales. It was midwinter cold and, apart from a few argumentative seagulls, a couple of thoughtfully resting cormorants and a magnificent sea eagle wheeling above me (perhaps wondering if I was a trifle too big for its beak), there were no other living creatures in the landscape. The chilled wind, coming off the Bass Strait, had whipped the sea into a series of choppy waves, which were breaking and surging over a parapet of rocks, before spreading into foaming rivulets across a stony beach below a low cliff. The light was fading fast and, although well rugged-up in my ancient duffel coat and cords, I shivered; remembering Matthew Arnold's 'Dover Beach', with its 'grating roar' of pebbles finding the 'eternal note of sadness' Sophocles had noticed on the Aegean long ago, suggesting it recalled 'the turbid ebb and flow of human misery'. Having been dragged along in the turbid flow of John Howard's miserable coalition for the past decade, my thoughts turned inwards, and I must warn you, dear reader – in the dulcet tones of an ABC announcer – the following lines contain some dark perceptions.

I've watched the mean-spirited paranoia and arrogant obsessions of the heartless Howard years unwind with an increasing sense of despair and shame, causing my faith in humanity to decline, perhaps irretrievably. If there had been no regime change, the calcification of Australia's bones would have been beyond repair, and our transformation into a selfish, anxious and suspicious nation, culturally drip-fed by America, and hopelessly addicted to economic rationalism and right-wing Christian fundamentalism, would have been achieved. And I, for one, don't wish to know about it. In such a place, books and writing would be further diminished. Already profoundly disappointed, I'm in questionable health and approaching the biblical use-by date. I'd be hard pressed to find motivation for much more than an occasional cup of tea and a cheese and chutney sandwich.

I've been brooding more than usual of late, partly because of the Howard factor, but also because of an increasingly painful reality associated with the double curse of trying to make my way in an extremely difficult job, which few people recognise as being a real job – that of writing – while living with the largely invisible handicap of an awful illness, which few people recognise as being a real illness – that of clinical depression. Since coming out of the closet, as it were, with my collection of stories, essays and poems, *Evening at Murunna Point*, which tries to get under the skin of depression through writing, I've become increasingly aware that if you lack celebrity status (which routinely attracts praise for having the 'courage' to openly face 'your demons') you'd be better off keeping quiet and copping it sweet. As I did for most of my life, before naively assuming *Evening at Murunna Point* might help erode some of the mystery and social stigma surrounding mental illness. The fact that copies forwarded to well-known, if not iconic, public figures with a self-evident degree of interest (for the psychological, as well as literary, aspects of the book) went unacknowledged was only part of the subsequent sense of isolation and despair in which I found myself trapped.

My writing has always sought to bridge the readership gap between so-called literary and popular ends of the market, and consequently runs the risk of going unnoticed by both. I'm proud that each of my four books achieved critical acceptance against the odds, and that my diverse portfolio of reviews, stories, poems and essays won praise and occasional awards, but now, in the face of advice from mainstream publishers about how 'beautifully' I write, although lacking a profile and commercial edge, they can't guarantee sufficient economic return, I'm burnt out, disenchanted and disillusioned. Frankly, I'd be more usefully occupied by starting a rare boot-lace collection.

I'm not being melodramatic; just fatalistic. I'm on the wing. And watching that sea eagle the other evening, the prospect doesn't sound too bad; even without a god, and therefore no promise of an afterlife. According to Bruce Chatwin in *Songlines*, the Bushmen of the Kalahari have no myths about survival in another world: 'When we die, we die,' they say, 'the wind blows away our footprints, and that is the end of us.' I'm happy to go along with that. All things considered – particularly the Howard government – it's just as well. Although there's always time for a few more words, aptly provided from the finishing lines of the poem I started out with:

> Ah, love, let us be true
> To one another! For the world, which seems
> To lie before us like a land of dreams,
> So various, so beautiful, so new,
> Hath really neither joy, nor love, nor light,
> Nor certitude, nor peace, nor help for pain;
> And we are here as on a darkling plain
> Swept with confused alarms of struggle and flight,
> Where ignorant armies clash by night.

Of waiting and whiskey

I was little more than a child, and waiting for a bus, when I first encountered the awful epiphany of knowing life to be fundamentally unfair, where promises are seldom kept; truth burns you alive; honesty doesn't prevent punishment; deception pays a dividend; heroes have feet of clay, and evil often wears a winning smile – where justice is a myth, and despair a cardinal sin.

The bus, when it eventually arrived, through the frozen light of an English winter, would take me on the first step of a long journey to the other side of the world; to the stark midsummer heat of Fremantle in Western Australia: the promised land of the ten-pound Pom.

I now realise – like Beckett – that life is defined by waiting; if not always for Godot, for exam results; for the kindness of strangers, or the redemption of a lover; for the birth of a child; the acceptance of an idea, or the easing of pain; and ultimately, of course, for the oblivion of escape.

I particularly remember waiting for the birth of my first child, a daughter, who was named Kerry – by Celtic whim – after a remote region of the west coast of Ireland, which I knew only from stories, but regarded as poetic heritage. Kerry was born in a small hospital in the Swan Valley, on the rural fringe of Perth. As my heavily pregnant wife disappeared, together with her pathetically battered suitcase, I was dismissed by a no-nonsense matron as being no longer required. Things were done differently then, and I went quietly, returning to our rented hovel (which is now, I noticed recently, a fashionably terraced and desirable suburban residence) to make myself a consoling cup of tea. And then to wait through the lonely, restless, and seemingly never-ending night, lamentably uninformed about the reality of birth, and struggling to accept, let alone understand, the nature of fatherhood.

When, next morning, bleary-eyed, and unwashed, I was led into a corridor with a long glass window, behind which stood a row of cots, each containing a raw pink baby, my bewildered gaze could barely focus in the direction of my daughter. Her eyes were closed but she was awake, her miniature hands moving in front of her face, as if already fending off the world. As I watched, spellbound with a complexity of emotion beyond my ability to unravel, I became fascinated by the exquisite but fearful beauty of her tiny fingers, each one tipped by an improbably minute but perfect fingernail. If there is a single aspect of us that captures human fragility more vividly than the hand of a new-born baby, then I would like to know what it is.

My wife was good at having babies, and we had three more in quick succession, before making a pragmatic reconciliation with our Catholic faith by deciding on birth control. Unsurprisingly, perhaps, we now have no faith; except in the decency, tolerance and compassion of our four adult children. For us, they are beacons of hope in an increasingly intolerant and dangerous world. Because today, more years after that distantly recalcitrant bus than I care to remember, I am still waiting – this time for an election result, with a glass of whiskey close to hand. Irish whiskey, spelt with an 'e', and releasing the mellow sadness of an Atlantic coastline, seen dimly in the Celtic twilight I tried to preserve by naming a daughter after one of its most wild and beautiful regions.

My wife, sensibly perhaps, doesn't drink whiskey (with or without an 'e') but thankfully this doesn't mean I have to drink it alone. I have a dear friend, even more ancient than me, who loves the stuff, although she prefers to drink it with enough ice to offend the meekest of Irishman. And so we sit together, my dear friend and I, in an Australian twilight, to sip our whiskey and consider the bleakness of a postmodern world, with its consummate madness of war; environmental vandalism of insatiable greed; arrogant stupidity of religious and economic fundamentalism; corruption of corporate and political expediency; but also, as the whiskey slips smoothly across the tongue, the healing redemption of poetry, music and laughter.

However, the prognosis isn't good. For countless ages the earth and the sun managed a reasonable homeostasis, which a few hundred years of industrial development, culminating in a period of relentless 'economic growth', has tipped towards catastrophe, perhaps irredeemably so, leaving only the bitter taste of profound frustration and despair at the way recent years have been wasted by argument and recrimination; by the way global warming has been doubted and denied; by the way money needed to help find a solution has been thrown at the empty arrogance of weapons and war – and ultimately, by the way all these things have betrayed future generations.

As I sip the last of my whiskey, salvation becomes hauntingly symbolised by an image of my daughter's fingers, shortly after her birth: tiny, fragile and precariously beautiful.

Post 2007 election footnote

Of course, I was pleased with the result, but couldn't help seeing it as curiously hollow, reflecting a desire for change that ignored the most important reasons. Where was the moral indignation about Iraq, Indigenous injustice, refugee policy, and global warming doubt and denial? Paul Keating's antique French clocks and Italian suits generated more anger than John Howard's lies. And already the dangerously fatuous myth about Howard being 'the best Australian prime minister' is threatening to become a millstone that will distort and corrupt future elections, crippling the new government's chances of winning back the kind of Australia we like to fondly remember as having once inhabited.

Of language and literature

I never got around to writing a satirical history of critical theory, despite years of muttering darkly about deconstructing postmodernism, whose vacuous arrogance has much to answer for, including harassing the intrinsic beauty of poetry – the mother tongue of language and literature – into the shameful oblivion of deliberately self-indulgent obscurity. Apart from the redeeming comfort of a few well-directed but unnoticed essays, the easy scorn of an odd angry review, or the self-conscious satisfaction of a piss-taking poem, I have – for reasons to do with existential inertia, profoundly frustrated disappointment, and sheer bloody boredom – let Ozlit's smugly internalised nepotism pass largely unchallenged. Which is a culpable shame.

Of course, as I have often said before, to achieve such a purpose, literature must be framed in an accessible language, which doesn't mean having to dumb down the canon by aiming at the lowest common denominator; it involves making people feel welcome, rather than excluded. The average punter reads banal books and consumes crass media, partly through being unaware of anything better, but mostly through having been made to feel unwanted when trying to access something better.

The arts have always tended to nourish a precious core, and Ozlit is no exception, with its increasingly risible cult of authorship. Of course, there are hard-working and honest exceptions, but many insiders, the ones oiling the gears that grind out this esoteric exclusivity – the literary academics; the so-called public intellectuals; the introverted and angst-ridden critics; the breathlessly self-obsessed and terminally precious poets; the high-minded editors, and all their fawning acolytes – are disinclined to worry about reaching beyond the sacred circle of their own kind. Like Pontius Pilate, they're likely to turn away and wash their hands, saying that if those outside the castle gates can't find the keys, it's nobody's fault but their own.

Perhaps some of you happened to read my colleague, Stephen Matthews, when he elegantly reviewed several arguments about whether the book was dead, dying or merely unwell, and noted that – apart from the vaporous prospect of electronic books in cyberspace – the cult of the celebrity had already affected the way people read books, becoming 'less open-minded' and requiring a book to be 'validated' by well-known opinion, presumably even if coming from a philistine. In fact, the word 'literary' is turning the reader away, which is depressing news if you happen to be – as I am – a writer of literary fiction.

I also review literary fiction, and usually enjoy novels written by good poets, because they're likely to care very much about words, and the manner in which they are used. And caring enough to get things right is one of the most important aspects of any art. If we are to survive the twenty-first century, language and literature will play vitally integral roles; not only because they enrich our imagination, which in turn allows us to see things in a more tolerant and compassionate way, but because they define us as a human species. At the last count, there were thought to be around six thousand languages in global existence, from which we still haven't managed to find one likely to allow us to communicate in a way that might reduce, let alone remove, poverty, cruelty and war.

Language is the scaffolding of literature; literature is the interpretation of culture, and culture is the expression of collective meaning. And collective meaning is the living, breathing core of humanity: the beginning and the end of everything. At least, as far as we wretched creatures are concerned. The act of choosing a good book, turning its pages, and entering its imagination, with an open mind, is just one step on the long journey towards a truly civilised reality. And a good book, a book that might be considered literature, is – in the final analysis – simply a book that cares enough about getting things right.

However, I guess caring about getting things right is just another casualty of this God-awful age of greed and instant gratification; of self-righteous war and blind prejudice; of economic and religious fundamentalisms; the politics of fear and paranoia; the dangerously fatuous cult of celebrity, and the possibly fatal neglect of our environment. And what do you think is carrying the enormous weight of this obscenely wasteful and arrogantly puffed-up nonsense? Little more than the empty vanity of our supposedly superior species status. Which demands an even bigger question, possibly the biggest of them all: do we deserve to survive? Not, I suggest, in our present, apparently remorseless, state. But then, what would I know? I'm just a grumpy old sod in the middle of a bad-hair week. And frankly, my dear, I'm beginning to suspect I don't give a damn.

Of folly and frustration

I was recently reading *The Guardian* in bed at three o'clock in the morning (as one does) when I came across a curiously jaundiced little piece about one of my favourite poets. There's a good chance you've heard of him, since he was once poet laureate; a man of complex sophistication, with a genuine love of architecture and landscape, plus a roughish eye for 'strapping' young gels of a certain English ilk. He is, or was – since he departed some time ago for that undiscovered poem from where no reader returns – Sir John Betjeman.

The *Guardian* piece, a brief column, scribbled, I suspect, on a napkin during a long literary lunch, noted the passing – at the grand old age of ninety-two – of Joan Hunter Dunn, whose girlish charms had brightened the dark days of World War Two for a youthful John Betjeman; inspiring 'A Subaltern's Love Song', which became, according to *The Guardian* scribbler, 'the most famous middle-brow love poem of the 20th century…containing lines close to doggerel'. An assertion apparently influenced by the 'final banality' of its closing couplet: 'We sat in the car park till twenty to one/And now I'm engaged to Miss Joan Hunter Dunn.' In fact, they were never engaged; the poem was a whimsical expression of delight at the distracting beauty of a young woman during London's wartime blitz, especially 'the tilt of her nose and the chime of her voice.' The lines are far from doggerel, and certainly not banal. They are quintessentially poetic.

John Betjeman's poetry contains lines of such silken cadence they slide across the tongue like vintage wine; sensuous, accessible and quotable; which is a damn sight more than can be said for most so-called poetry produced today – and I use the word 'produced' advisedly, since much of it seems likely to have come from a test-tube fragment of cerebral cortex rather than the pen (or keyboard) of a living, breathing person, passionately beset (or besotted) with life. Poets are a flawed bunch, some more so than others, and Sir John was certainly no exception. At least he had the good grace to acknowledge the condition. Near the end of his life, a seriously intense but comely young female BBC TV arts journalist wound up a highbrow literary interview by asking if the great man had any regrets. There was a long and loaded pause, as everyone waited for a few final words of poetic wisdom. Then, shifting slightly in his comfortable studio chair, Sir John gazed wistfully at the beautiful young woman in front of him, and replied with a wry smile, 'I would like to have had time for more sex.'

We tend to forget, in our elevated moments of self-appraisal, that we are merely creatures of flesh and blood, driven more by biological instinct than the supposedly superior intelligence of a tenuously grasped civilisation, and I suggest Sir John, with a mischievous twinkle in his eye, was reminding us of this folly.

On a wider, bleaker and more recent canvas, we need look no further than the monstrous folly of the Iraq war, with its consequent global frustration, to see the premise still holding true. For example, the self-serving and Machiavellian deceit of Donald Rumsfeld is sufficiently of the same magnitude as that of Osama Bin Laden to demonstrate the evil of their collective stance without even considering the obscenity of all the wasted lives, time and money summoned by accumulated hatred between Islamic fundamentalism and right-wing Christian arrogance. And the sheer frustration of having to suffer the drip-fed euphemisms and evasions of a profoundly damaged political system, coupled with the self-serving rhetoric of a generally right-wing media commentary, invites deep despair.

Of course, the corrosive effects of such hubris flourish in the hot-house world of celebrity opinion makers. The apparently untouchable shock-jock Alan Jones accused ABC TV's *Media Watch* of 'bile and bias' for having the cheek to report that his radio broadcast of a well-worn urban myth about refugees getting more government assistance than pensioners was a lie. Typically, Alan blustered his way out of the charge, before spewing his own poisonous bile at the ABC for being a bunch of lay-about, tired old lefties. Great balls of celestial fire! Will no one rid us of this meddlesome prat? Probably not, because the commercial interests behind his appalling program know the credulous punters love him. His world, it would seem, casts an awful shadow of where and who we are, and of how and why we constitute reality by answering questions we haven't even begun to understand.

The process is reinforced across the entire community; look at the spiteful politics behind the Olympics, or the glittering vulgarity of twenty-twenty cricket in India (if ever there was a more appropriate metaphor for today's rampant consumerism of greed, speed and synthetic values, then I must have missed it). Seventy years ago, the BBC cricket commentator, John Arlott, captured the poetic charm of real cricket with these lines:

> Sunburnt fieldsmen, flannelled cream,
> looked, though urgent, scarce alive,
> swooped, like swallows of a dream,
> on skimming fly, the hard hit drive.

With apologies to John Arlott (who I admired as a writer, poet and cricket lover) I'll close with some lines that attempt to describe the ugly mayhem of the twenty-twenty version of a great game:

> Fast food fieldsmen, preened obscene,
> looked, though hungry, over-ripe,
> lunged like vultures from a scream,
> on killer-wasp, the tortured swipe.

Of morality and manners

A powerful scene from one of my favourite movies has Orson Welles (in the character of Harry Lime, from Graham Greene's bleak thriller *The Third Man*) delivering these memorable lines to suggest that immorality is more profitable than good manners:

> In Italy for thirty years under the Borgias they had warfare, terror, murder and bloodshed, but they produced Michelangelo, Leonardo da Vinci and the Renaissance. In Switzerland they had brotherly love – they had five hundred years of democracy and peace, and what did that produce? The cuckoo clock.

A clever piece of rhetoric, despite the doubtful accuracy of its historic analogy: the cuckoo clock was a German invention, and the Swiss were (and almost certainly still are) just as prone to the fallibility of human nature as the rest of us. And the moral vacuum of those responsible for our recent financial meltdown certainly wasn't profitable for most people.

In fact, the capitalist ethic of letting the market take care of its own mistakes sounds embarrassingly hollow in the wake of democratic governments having to use public funds to bail out private loss. The trouble with financial politics being so profoundly mortgaged to capitalist greed is the commensurate belief that there is no problem that cannot be solved by simply throwing enough money at it. Frankly, I wish someone would throw this meltdown into a hole and bury it, along with all the Harry Lime crooks who helped orchestrate the sorry mess, unforgivably distracting the world from what should be its primary focus at the moment: a meltdown of cataclysmically different dimension – that of global warming.

Personally, I've never seen much purpose for money beyond that of spending it, and regard most forms of financial investment (except those involved with regulated superannuation, or other well-mannered aims) as being merely an extension of gambling. I write essays, book reviews and occasional poetry, regarding this occupation as a contribution (however small) to the cultural well-being of the community; for which I am paid a pittance. Whereas a pin-stripped financial zealot, zapping vast amounts of money around the world, sometimes so fast it doesn't even touch the ground, gets a king's ransom. To consider the morality and manners of this absurdly unbalanced equation, is, I suggest, to open an insight on the core of our present malaise: a kind of creeping cultural separatism, where people are increasingly inclined to simply not care if others aren't keeping up; not necessarily because they can't, or don't want to, but because they somehow don't measure up, by failing to tick the boxes in a way that might satisfy the gate keepers.

With honourable exceptions, contemporary poetry has been chased into a backwater by esoteric self-indulgence (akin to Wall Street) that couldn't give a dactyl's toe whether art is drifting beyond the reach of the ordinary punter. And this is a tragedy, since our increasingly complex and dangerous world needs access to poetic imagination in order to think beyond the point where money, guns or diplomacy have failed. Over a daunting stretch of human history, we've become an adaptable and resilient species, with scientific and technological advance keeping us ahead of diverse threat, but the twenty-first century is shaping as the ultimate test. If we can safely get through the next one hundred years, our long-term future will be secure, because we will have fixed problems far greater than financial meltdown.

We're going to need a level of imagination, morality and manners capable of generating the collective will to cooperate; in a sense of constructive sharing, rather than destructive self-interest. And the key to achieving this won't be found in the chaotic greed of Wall Street; religious and imperial fundamentalisms; or even the brightest of economic think tanks. Finding an answer to global warming will generate its own economy, more socially inclusive than the current version, and our long-term survival will depend on the lateral thinking of a new political mantra: 'It's the environment, stupid!'

The proposition is so obvious; it fills me with despair to hear opinion-makers claim the economy always comes first. Are they simply dumb? Or so selfish they don't care what happens to subsequent generations? I've said this before in these pages, so forgive me for saying it again, clearly: we can have an environment without an economy, but we can't have an economy without an environment.

Sadly, the architects of this latest financial meltdown know little of the complex synergies connecting humanity, and care even less. Their focus is as esoteric (and empty) as postmodern poetry. Their lives won't be sacrificed. The pin-stripped financial zealot in front of a computer screen zapping mythical money to God knows where will be okay; it's the people doing real work – the kind that actually produces something – who will suffer. I hope they're inclined to think in terms of renewal, rather than revenge. The global money market has always favoured self-interest over community interest. Perhaps being more concerned with sharing success (as opposed to loss) might allow capitalism a usefully productive role in a post-apocalyptic world.

Postscript

Late on Sunday, 2 November I watched a broadcast of Rupert Murdoch's 2008 Boyer Lecture on ABC TV. The tedium of capitalist cliché, coupled with bottom-line belief in endless economic growth, was occasionally interrupted by recognition of the bleedin' obvious, and could have been delivered by Joe the plumber. But the seemingly mesmerised audience hung on every word as if receiving profound wisdom; demonstrating, yet again, that who you are matters more than what you say, and confirms the current monopoly of celebrity public opinion; which comes back to the need to democratise social and cultural comment. Come on, give it a go…

Of heroism and hubris

In childhood we live under the brightness of immortality – heaven is as near and actual as the seaside. Behind the complicated details of the world stand the simplicities: God is good, the grown-up man or woman knows the answer to every question, there is such a thing as truth, and justice is as measured and faultless as a clock. Our heroes are simple: they are brave, they tell the truth, they are good swordsmen and they are never really defeated. That is why no later books satisfy us like those which were read to us in childhood – for those promised a world of great simplicity of which we knew the rules, but later books are complicated and contradictory with experience; they are formed out of our own disappointing memories – of the VC in the police-court dock, of the faked income tax return, the sins in corners, and the hollow voice of the man we despised talking to us of courage and purity. The Little Duke is dead and betrayed and forgotten; we cannot recognise the villain and we suspect the hero and the world is small cramped place. The two great popular statements of faith are 'What a small place the world is' and 'I'm a stranger here myself.'

Graham Greene, *The Ministry of Fear* (1943)

My childhood heroes included Dennis Compton, Alfred Lord Tennyson and a high school English teacher (whose name escapes my memory but whose inclination to read my essays and stories aloud to my classmates – who usually received them in sullen silence – certainly does not). A life time later, I have no heroes, although I'm prepared to accept that Trooper Mark Donaldson deserved his Victoria Cross; a belief gratifyingly confirmed by his unselfish response to the award, suggesting he might be a good bloke as well as a hero.

On the other hand, I'm appalled by Federal Opposition frontbencher Tony Abbott's suggestion of a comparably heroic status for our former prime minister, John Howard, a man palpably disgraced by years of disingenuous leadership, opportunistic immorality and insufferable hubris. 'Only a fool would accept a medal from an idiot,' someone cheerfully observed from the sideline of Tony Abbot's online bilious blog concerning Dubya's parting gift to his little Aussie mate. This appeared to summarise the incident rather nicely, except for the fact that John Howard may be many things, most of which don't bear close examination, but he is certainly no fool; which, of course, places his sins – of omission and commission – in an altogether higher league of political bastardry.

'I did what I thought was right' appears to be the default response from those tired old warhorses once collectively known as the Coalition of the Willing, as if the glib emptiness of the phrase might exonerate a degree of criminality that arguably should have placed them before International Courts of Justice. In fact, the British television movie on Tony Blair, shown on ABC TV, explored precisely that scenario, although the satire was sufficiently heavy-handed to detract from what might have otherwise comprised a usefully informed psycho-political drama. If the catastrophic debacle of Iraq wasn't enough to warrant John Howard's indictment, then the terminally bankrupt morality of his government's cruelly incompetent refugee policy; dangerously recalcitrant climate change dithering (if not denial), and a patronising and culturally disruptive invasion of Northern Territory Indigenous sovereignty surely would. In any event, they all conspire to illustrate what a monstrously offensive joke his post-prime ministerial global hero posturing has become.

I guess it's easy for political spin and a complicit media to mitigate the intrinsic shame of such matters, but common humanity – if nothing else – requires John Howard's history as Australian prime minister to be seen in the cold hard light of day, rather than the fuzzy twilight of reconstituted neo-conservatism, or the addled memories of right-wing sycophants like Tony Abbott. The seemingly unquenchable hubris of Australian conservatives has never ceased to amaze me, but this time I wonder if it is merely the 'born-to-rule' syndrome at work, or a reflection of some deeper political flaw based on our risibly adversarial party system. Despite having been soundly defeated at the last federal election, members of the new opposition continue to behave as if they'd been the unfortunate victims of a ballot-box aberration rather than rejected by an electorate that finally grew weary of their mean-spirited arrogance, and decided to vote for something better.

We are products of our history. The nineteenth century built empires, which the twentieth century demolished, producing the rubble that provided fertile ground for the growth of noxious weeds like fundamentalism and hubris. Religious faith is based on irrational belief, but still forms the focus of our search for collective meaning. The distance between faith and reason is as near, or as far, as that between knowledge and wisdom, and our desire to create order often creates chaos. In this supposedly enlightened age, many people still believe absolute nonsense. In fact, much of what we believe today often stands in stark contrast to the truth (insofar as that can ever be known) and it will take a twenty-first century super-hero to deliver us from darkness. We're more likely to find one by casting out hubris, rediscovering imagination and adopting a little humility.

Of racism and reality

I was in a taxi recently, up front next to the driver in deference to a lifelong sense of egalitarianism rather than my instinctive social reticence, when the desultory conversation stumbled towards Indigenous affairs. (I don't do small talk very well, quickly becoming discomforted by taxi drivers, hairdressers or fellow travellers in general.)

Anyway, this taxi driver, a nice old guy, who I could easily imagine being someone's favourite uncle, said, apropos of not very much, 'There are three things you can't give an Aborigine.' Apprehensively, I waited for the punchline, which came with a self-satisfied smirk: 'A broken nose, a fat lip and a job.'

My stony silence seemed to puzzle him; apparently he was used to getting a laugh from what he obviously considered a witty observation, and tried a few other gossipy gambits, all of which I let pass through to the keeper.

Reaching my destination, mercifully nearby, I paid him without comment (or tip) and turned away, regretting I hadn't been quick-witted enough to reply, 'And there's one thing you can't give a stupidly prejudiced taxi driver – a brain.' Although this would have been unfair, as well as untrue, since clearly he wasn't stupid.

In reality, the nature of racism has more to do with deeply ingrained and unjustified assumptions than stupidity, although racists are generally unaware of their racism, in much the same way as stupid people are unaware of their stupidity.

The crux of racism is its iceberg effect: the essential dynamic of the beast lives below the surface, waiting for the right (or wrong) moment, or set of triggering circumstances, to inflict its damage. And let's be clear about this: covert racism, of the routinely casual, everyday type – as displayed by my basically good-natured taxi driver – is more dangerous than the overt, straight-in-your-face variety, which usually does imply a functionally impaired cerebral cortex. Covert racists are likely to be deeply offended – as I'm sure my taxi driver would have been – if challenged. Their flawed assumptions can creep over a community, like a virus, or rust on the garden gate, until they have assumed, by a kind of osmosis, a culture of otherness; an accepted sense of superiority and inferiority. The process is easily tracked: pigmentation produces prejudice; difference implies danger and the unknown; what we cannot, or will not, understand, we learn to fear; what we fear we grow to hate, and what we hate we sooner or later seek to destroy.

If the cause of racism is so apparent, why can't we fix it? Sadly, that part is not so easy, perhaps because the human condition is predisposed towards prejudice in much the same way as it is towards irrational belief.

There's a tiny but vividly revealing passage in Ted Egan's excellent book *Justice All Their Own*, when an Arnhem Land Aborigine is taken to Darwin in the 1930s and climbs a set of steps on his hands and knees. The action is either confirmation of his subhuman status or a reasonable response to a confusing and totally unknown object others had learned to take for granted. The wrong assumption was made back then and is still being made to this day, in variously institutionalised forms of racist behaviour all over Australia. In an age of sophisticated reason and technology, we remain afraid of the dark, the bogeyman; the primordial superstitions of the stone age. It's time we grew up and recognised racism for what it really is: an unjustified assumption of superiority based on ignorance and fear.

When our newly elected prime minister, Kevin Rudd, delivered a long-overdue apology to Indigenous Australians, there was a palpable sense of relief; of something having taken place that might actually assist reconciliation and reduce the insidious undercurrent of racism; particularly in rural Australia. Sadly, this doesn't seem to have happened.

I live near Bermagui, a pleasant little fishing village on the far south coast of NSW. Despite being a culturally rich and artistic community, the region is experiencing the ugly fallout from a series of senseless and vicious racist attacks on a decent and well-known Indigenous family, the details of which appear to have been deliberately suppressed by public authorities, and played down or ignored by local media. This shameful episode illustrates how the covert racism of a few people in positions of power and influence can be used to deflect and mitigate the mindless cruelty of overt racism. In recent years, we have been encouraged to believe that racism in rural Australia has declined, but events in the sea-change town of Bermagui suggest that the reality is tragically different.

Racism is totally irrational and utterly indefensible. Its toxic reality is a cancer of the human condition, nourished by the half-light and darkness of the urban myth, and must be fully exposed to the hard light of day by constant public scrutiny, facilitated by a free and independent media; so that everyone can see the under-handed, mean-spirited and spiteful way it works to diminish us all.

Epilogue

I've always loved words – the sounds, patterns and meanings they can make – although, since the well-received appearance of my third novel, a couple of decades ago, I've produced mostly words about words from other people (in the form of book reviews or literary criticism) rather than any more books of my own. There are many reasons for this; including the economic rationalism and narrowing arteries of mainstream publishing; but, in my case, it's also sadly to do with an increasing crisis of self-confidence (fuelled largely by distressingly persistent anxiety disorder and clinical depression) coupled strongly with the suspicion that there are already too many books for a relatively limited Australian readership market.

This essay selection (the literati may rankle at the category definition, but I'll use it anyway) was ditheringly nagged into being by passionate belief in social justice, democracy, and freedom to express ideas that often criticise political authority. Like many people today, I'm appalled by the creeping tide of holier-than-thou, right-wing Christianity and Islamic fundamentalism currently shaping a global conflict that increasingly distracts us from the bigger picture of long-term environmental well-being and survival, and if these pieces (no, damn it, these essays) can somehow help provide a critically thoughtful backdrop for larger ideas, then I shall be satisfied with their appearance in this form. They span part of the Howard years, and reflect my deep despair at his disingenuous leadership, steeped as it was in the selfish paranoia of fundamentally materialistic values.

But this isn't about left-wing reactions (the GetUp! campaign – among others – clearly indicated much wider disaffection); it's about trying to reclaim Australia as the country we always assumed it to be: decent, fair-minded and easy-going.

I.M.
Beauty Point (Wallaga Lake), NSW
Spring 2009

www.ingramcontent.com/pod-product-compliance
Lightning Source LLC
Chambersburg PA
CBHW021838020426
42334CB00014B/694